PORTFOLIO A

METROPOLITAN SEMINARS IN ART

Great Periods in Painting

PORTFOLIO A

Glory and Grandeur: THE CLASSICAL BACKGROUND

BY JOHN CANADAY

ART EDITOR AND CRITIC
THE NEW YORK TIMES

THE METROPOLITAN MUSEUM OF ART

GLORY AND GRANDEUR

The Classical Background

ESTHETICIANS have theorized for centuries about the source of the creative instinct and the disciplines that guide it, but only recently has art stopped being something the average person could enjoy spontaneously and become, instead, a kind of puzzle to be explained.

In earlier, more unified civilizations than ours, art expressed a point of view as acceptable to the man in the street as to the man in the palace or church who commissioned the work and to the man in the workshop who created it. The man in the medieval street had no quarrel with the design of the Gothic cathedral because it was "too modern," though it represented a radical break with what went before. And when Giotto revolutionized painting (Portfolio 8, Plates 89 and 90), people were not puzzled or scandalized by what he was doing. They marveled.

But when times get as complex and out of kilter as they have been for the past hundred years, the relationship between the artist and the observer gets out of kilter too. Each may be in tune with the times, yet out of tune with the other. This estrangement has been called "the divorce between civilization and culture," civilization being a practical and social way of life, and culture its intellectual and artistic expression. This divorce of a pair that had suffered only minor disagreements during a marriage of many thousands of years is a tragedy of our day. "Art appreciation," the concern of these Seminars, is an attempt at reconciliation through an intermediary.

The difficulty is increased because we are surrounded by the accumulated art of the past as well as by the proliferating art of the moment, and we want to understand everything at once. The portfolios of the first series of Seminars were concerned with general principles, without much regard to chronology. The second series will enlarge our acquaintance with the art of the past (and the present) by taking up different periods in historical sequence. Painting will continue to be our main subject, but sculpture and architecture will receive some attention in the early portfolios.

We are beginning a history of art as the expression of ideas that have been tributaries to the mainstream of thought in the Western world. These tributaries are innumerable, but the principal ones are: the intellectual idealism of the ancient world, the Christian mysticism of the Middle Ages, and the rational, objective investigation of natural phenomena that began with the Renaissance and developed into the age of science.

We are concerned in this portfolio with the fountainhead of Western civilization—"the glory that was Greece and the grandeur that was Rome," as Edgar Allan Poe described our romantic vision of classical antiquity.

The Dream of Greece

Ancient Greece, as we have grown to visualize it from its ruined architecture, its broken statues, its heroic legends, and its fragments or

5

echoes of painting, is a dream, a romantic vision of a few perfect islands and a golden shore, washed by perfumed seas, inhabited by a race of men and women with bodies perfectly formed, eternally young, of godlike grace, moving among blanched temples glistening pure in the sun on rocky promontories. When death enters this world it is heroic, majestic. Even war is a kind of Olympic game, a magnificently staged display of prowess between naked athletes bearing brazen shields. If men suffer and die, they do so in attitudes as beautiful and noble as those we are familiar with in sculpture.

Common sense tells us that this dream could not be true; it would tell us so even if antiquity had not left other records that deny it. Life in the ancient world was normally imperfect, normally subject to chance and misfortune. Wars were murderous, maiming, and cruel— as they have always been. Old age, sickness, ugliness, vice, intolerance, corruption, and stupidity existed—as they always have.

But Greek life and thought were ennobled and unified by a great conviction, the conviction that man on earth was capable of formulating and achieving an ideal state of being. This ideal of perfection is so pervasively expressed in Greek art that we think of it as having been, indeed, achieved in Greek life. But perhaps this is only as it should be: art is the tangible form men give to the ideas they live by; these inner realities are more important than any historical details of circumstantial evidence that seem to modify or contradict them. The art of ancient Greece remains for us the immortal recall of a glorious age.

Gods and Heroes

The world that was to evolve, disappear, and emerge once more as our dream of antiquity began some five thousand years ago on the island of Crete, near the Greek mainland. About 700 B.C. it entered a period of rise that climaxed three hundred years later in the Golden Age of Athens. From the first, this civilization had an exuberance, a love of life, an inventiveness, a curiosity, enthusiasm, and flexibility that set it apart from other ancient civilizations. It was a civilization in which the individual counted for something, where life demanded ingenuity and initiative. In Egypt, by contrast, the self-sufficiency of the land permitted a despotic king-god-priest to impose his will on a small upper class and a mass of peasants and slaves. Egyptian life and thought, and hence art, were so static that its formulas were repeated for three thousand years. Egyptian art has its special fascinations, and it has variations within the limits of the formulas, but it is not a part of Western man's tremendous adventure of self-discovery, which is the essence of the history of art. The long and placid story of Egyptian art is like a journey along the Nile; the Greeks take us onto the sparkling sea.

The life of Greece and its islands depended on seafarers, warriors, and adventurers, not on docile peasants; it depended on men of energy and imagination who were not likely to prostrate themselves before arbitrary authority. The heroes of Greek legend and history are men who offer respectful alliance, not humble subservience, to kings and even to gods. Greek religion developed as one in which gods were half men, and great men were half gods.

Is the *Kouros* (Plate A1, *Figures 1 and 2*) a god or a man? He is neither, and both. The statue commemorates an athlete awarded semidivine status by his fellow Greeks; his tomb was made a place of worship and his soul given a form of eternal life.

The Greeks appear to have held only a nominal belief in an afterlife for the rank and file of mankind. Their legends include a kind of hell called Tartarus and a kind of heaven called the Elysian fields, but the common afterworld was Hades, a shadowy subterranean region where souls existed forever in dreary forgetfulness. For the Greeks, no heaven could offer a joy greater than life fully lived; Hades was a kind of hell only because it was not the glorious world itself. In one legend Odysseus visits Hades and encounters the shade of the hero Achilles, who says, "I would rather be the basest slave on earth than a prince among the dead."

Greek love of life, which made man the measure of all things, explains the adulation of athletes. The Greeks adored man as a total being, and the athlete, in the perfection of his physical being, symbolized an intellectual and moral ideal. His control of his body was identified with discipline and clarity of mind; his physical beauty was a parallel to moral probity and intellectual harmony. That is why the *Kouros* could share a place of honor in the agora, or town market place and center, with the greatest warriors and the greatest lawmakers. It explains too why the history of Greek sculpture is so largely a history of sculpture of the human body.

The Archaic Style

Before we discuss the *Kouros* further, it would be a good idea to look at a parallel series of male and female statues (*Figures 3-8*) that constitute a thumbnail survey of Greek sculpture at its beginning, at its climax, and at the point where its spirit began to change in response to changing social conditions and ideals.

Now, by most people's standards, both series progress from a rather stiff, unrealistic style to "better" and "more beautiful" representation. The *Kouros* (*Figure 3*) and the *Maiden* from the Acropolis (*Figure 6*) belong to the Archaic period, about 625 to 480 B.C. (or to 450 B.C., if we include a transitional period). The second pair, the *Spear Bearer* (*Figure 4*) and an *Amazon* (*Figure 7*), are from the Golden Age, between 450 and 400 B.C. They follow the ideal proportions for human figures formulated by the sculptor Polyclitus. (The *Spear Bearer*, or *Doryphoros*, is an ancient copy of a lost original by Polyclitus; the

Figure 1   *Figure 2*

Amazon, an ancient copy of a lost statue attributed to Cresilas.) The "Canon of Polyclitus" established a ratio of the parts of the body based on mathematical multiples of a unit, such as a finger or a hand; the ideal proportion of the head to the figure, for instance, was one to seven. Ideal, of course, does not mean average, but in general Polyclitus' canon is a formulation of the normal proportions of a beautifully made human being.

The third pair, *Hermes with the Infant Dionysus* (*Figure 5*) and *Aphrodite of Cnidus* (*Figure 8*), are from the fourth century B.C., when Greece had passed its zenith as an integrated civilization and had entered a period marked by a certain relaxation of ideals and, in art, by a greater emphasis on purely sensuous beauty. The male figure, by Praxiteles

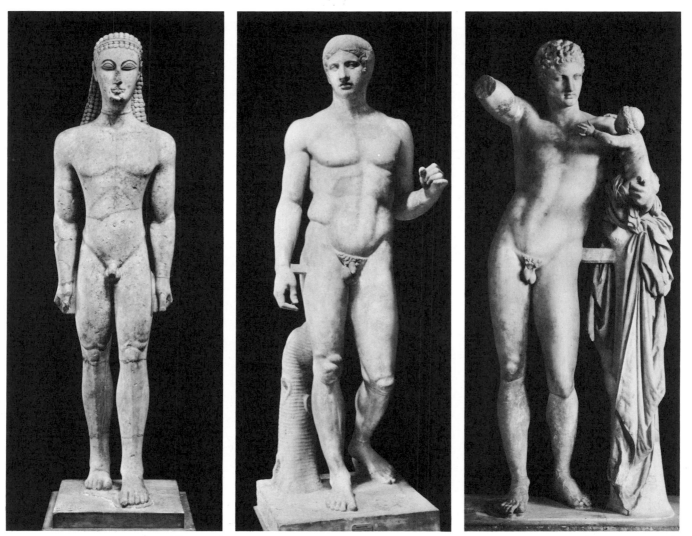

Figure 3 ^{Alinari}   *Figure 4* ^{Alinari}   *Figure 5*

(worked about 370-330 B.C.), is the only original Greek sculpture by a major artist to have come down to us. The female figure is a copy or a variation of his lost *Aphrodite of Cnidus*, by far the most admired work of its time, the most copied and imitated over a period of centuries, and the direct ancestor of the *Aphrodite* (Plate A2) we pair for contrast with the *Kouros* (Plate A1).

It is possible to consider the *Kouros*, which was carved some three hundred years before the *Aphrodite*, as the primitive effort of a sculptor working at a time when knowledge of the construction of the body and ways of representing it was inadequate for the creation of a great work of art. But the preceding portfolios should have taught us that expressive power can triumph over technical limitations,

that accurate imitation is not the goal of art. It is perfectly true that the *Kouros* is rigid in attitude, that the sculptor, lacking full knowledge of how to represent anatomy, employs conventions such as the disklike knees, the scalloplike indications of muscles above them, the strong ridges at the groin, and the stylized geometrical patterns of eyelids, brows, and hair. But these conventions are used with a feeling for organic unity, with an order and rhythm that give the statue an extraordinary completeness. The *Kouros* is filled with a sense of life so vital that it gives spiritual animation to physical forms held in check by the stone. Undeniably the stone still imposes its will on this early sculptor, so much so that we remain quite conscious of the block from which the statue was carved. But the sculptor in turn has

8

Alinari *Figure 6*   *Figure 7* Alinari   *Figure 8*

infused the stone with the magic of life, a life impatient for further release. The *Kouros* speaks to us of an age still primitive, but an age heroic, vigorous, and idealistic—a primitive age, but in no way a savage one.

In our day the attraction of primitive and archaic forms has been heightened, in a kind of reverse reaction, by the sophistications of modernism. The geometrical premise of much modern art was stimulated in part by a new appreciation of the geometrical forms in archaic art. Its vigor, conviction, and self-sufficiency appeal to artists who feel a lack of these qualities in the conventional painting and sculpture of our century. Thus Amedeo Modigliani (1884-1920), when he carved *Stone Head* (*Figure 9*) in a Paris studio, turned to primitive African and archaic Greek forms as

his point of departure; their unquenched vitality sustained him in the weariness and confusion of his world. In *The Kiss* (*Figure 10*), Constantin Brancusi (born 1876) went back even further to the roughest and crudest forms of pre-Greek carvings, using only a few shallow indications to break the surface of his stone block, synthesizing limitations that no longer existed.

The attraction of archaic forms for modern artists should show us, if nothing else does, that the very limitations under which the sculptor of the *Kouros* had to work contributed to the statue's special expressive character. By the operation of a natural law of esthetics, forms appropriate to the expression of an age are imposed by the nature of the materials and techniques at the artist's command.

9

Fulfillment of the Ideal

Between the *Kouros* and the *Spear Bearer* (*Figure 4*) there were many intermediate steps. Greek civilization was developing in every aspect, growing and opening until in Athens in the fifth century B.C. it flowered with a fullness and a unity paralleling the city's material well-being under the statesman Pericles (about 495-429 B.C.).

This was the Golden Age. In art the fusion of realism and idealism only suggested in the *Kouros* was finally achieved. The *Spear Bearer*, after Polyclitus, who was active from 450 to 420 B.C., is free of archaic strictures. The figure stands naturally and seems capable of movement, in contrast to the rigid stance of the *Kouros*. Anatomical structure is not only accurately represented but all the parts are logically articulated. Perfected craftsmanship enabled Polyclitus to state fully the ideal toward which the sculptor of the *Kouros* was taking the first steps. The canon of proportions formulated by Polyclitus is important only because it reflected the ideal of harmony by which man hoped to achieve his full potential as a being on this earth.

The dominant creative genius of the Golden Age was not Polyclitus, however, but Phidias (about 500-432 B.C.). In 449 B.C. Phidias conceived and supervised a program to make Athens the most beautiful city of all time. It may be a little disillusioning to learn that Pericles financed the project by diverting funds belonging to the Athenian Naval Confederacy, but to this manipulation we owe the existence of the temple to Athena called the Parthenon (*Figure 11*), the climactic expression of the Greek spirit. It was designed under Phidias' inspiration by the architects Ictinus and Callicrates.

To visit the Acropolis, the upward-thrusting mass of rock in the middle of Athens on which the ruins of the Parthenon stand, is an experience some tourists may be able to take in their stride. It is an experience that, conceivably,

Figure 9

some people might find disappointing. But for anybody with even an elementary feeling for the place of ancient Greece in our lives, the Acropolis is an experience of the most thrilling kind. Modern Athens is a big, not very beautiful, rather difficult city. (Ancient Athens by comparison was hardly more than a village.) The Acropolis swarms with sight-seers and must be approached through ranks of postcard and souvenir sellers. Yet it is immune to vulgarization. Its shattered buildings and ruined stones impose something of their original spirit on the most casual visitor. Fewer of the usual antics take place on the Acropolis than at other tourist highspots; it is quieter there. One is taken back to the morning of the world and, surprisingly, is impressed less with the antiquity of the ruins than with their wonderful immortality, their life and their youth.

10

The Parthenon itself, the major monument on the Acropolis and the great temple of the ancient world, is not so much a building as it is a piece of abstract sculpture, a study in pure proportion. In its original condition, with its individual stones perfectly joined, it must have appeared to have been carved from a single enormous block of marble. The Parthenon was conceived as a piece of exterior architecture— that is, as a beautiful object, a kind of altar, to be seen from the outside. The interior was divided into two chambers, a small one used as a treasury and a large one housing a gigantic gold and ivory statue of Athena. The ceremonial use of the interior was important, but even with a solid core the Parthenon would have been the perfect monument to the goddess of wisdom, dominating her city and reminding the Athenians, by the abstract logic and clarity of its design, that they were dedicated to a rational and balanced way of life. We still feel this quality in the Parthenon; what we are inclined to forget is that the building was once as joyous as it is noble, sparkling with the gold of its ornaments and the bright color of its painted sculpture. The effect is partially recaptured in reconstructions (*Figure 12*) made from records and deductions.

The Parthenon had already suffered cruel misfortunes when it was more then half destroyed in an explosion in 1687, while this noblest legacy of antiquity was being used by the Turks as a powder magazine. In succeeding years the sculpture was further ruined by vandalism and unsuccessful efforts to remove it from the pediments. Finally, most of the battered remaining pieces were successfully lowered from their positions high on the building by Lord Elgin and taken in 1806 to England, where they remain today in the British Museum. In the chilly gray light of London, mounted as exhibits, they still exude some of the radiance of the Athens of twenty-five hundred years ago.

The hero *Dionysus* (*Figure 13*) and the majestic *Three Fates* (*Figure 14*) were secondary

Figure 10

figures in the pedimental compositions of the Parthenon, but they evoke the fullness, the ceremonial rhythms, the monumental serenity, and the flowing harmonies of the many-figured scene. On one pediment is represented the birth of Athena and, on the other, her contest with the sea god Poseidon for sponsorship of the city. The pediment sculptures were planned by Phidias but not executed by him; his own contribution was the gold and ivory statue of the goddess inside the Parthenon. Not a fragment of the statue remains, but its approximate character is known through several varying copies.

The loftiness and sublimity of the Parthenon figures implies a certain impersonality. Intimate worldliness would have been out of place in the balance of the real and the ideal by which gods were endowed with human warmth

11

and human beings were endowed with divine dignity. Features are generalized, expressions are reserved, withdrawn. The head, in fact, is not essential to the expressive character of these gods and heroes except as a unit in a set of harmonious proportions ennobling the human body as a symbol of the nobility of the human spirit.

The beauty of the Parthenon sculpture cannot escape us, but that does not mean that we fully understand it. We see the grace of the bodies, we feel some of their serenity, but that is only the beginning. We must perceive the strength, the decision, of this sculpture.

The Greeks were strong in their convictions, unwilling to compromise or to gloss over uncertainties. They wanted passionately to know, to understand, and then to express this knowledge and understanding harmoniously, without exaggeration. We must remind ourselves again and again that this sculpture came from

a civilization that was investigating man against the background of a primitive age, rather than, as we do, against a background of the rise and fall of successive civilizations. The Greeks, seeing only consistent progress from primitivism toward the ideal, could conceive of man's attaining ultimate perfection. They wanted completeness, not suggestion—fulfillment, not novelty. They accepted limitation as a principle of art because it was necessary for the concise and absolute definition of things.

It is easy enough to set these ideas down in a few words, but it is more difficult, perhaps impossible, for us to realize what they mean in terms of a way of life and thought so far removed from our own. One detail, which may seem trivial in itself, illuminates an important aspect of Greek thought: the Parthenon figures were carved in the full round, including the backs, although the backs would not be seen

12

when the sculpture was in place on the temple. The passion for completeness, for unity, for total harmony, was so basic that to leave any part of the figures rough and uncarved would have violated the Greek faith in the ideal of self-contained truth. Possibly the most important quality in the Parthenon sculpture is this wholeness, this completeness. If we understand this aspect of Greek sculpture, we have gone a long way toward understanding the Greek ideal, an ideal that applied to the individual and to society, and hence, to art.

The Descent of the Gods

The spirit of the Golden Age could not endure for long. In the following century the golden balance became weighted on the side of lesser human values. The gods and heroes descended from their elevated positions to experiment with human pleasures. They retained a godlike beauty. They remained aristocrats, removed from the rank and file of humankind. But they were no longer divine.

Praxiteles' *Hermes* (*Figure 5*), carved about a hundred years after the Parthenon sculptures, is certainly one of the most beautiful pieces of sculpture, representing one of the most beautiful human bodies ever carved. The head (*Figure 15*) is of the utmost dreamy,

seductive, sensuous attraction. To hold any reservation whatsoever as to its consummate loveliness must seem niggling. But a reservation is usually made: for all its special perfections, the Praxitelean ideal is more entrancing than noble, more alluring than majestic, more enjoyable in sensuous terms than inspiring in intellectual ones. The Parthenon figures are expressions of an abstract ideal represented by tangible, godlike beings. The *Hermes*, by comparison, is a beautiful being who only secondarily may be associated with some higher ideal than physical beauty.

These comparisons are dangerous because they tend to become ratings of merit. The history of art is not a contest between the styles of one century and another. We point out the difference between the conception of sculpture of the Golden Age and that of Praxiteles in the fourth century B.C. to increase our understanding, and hence our enjoyment, of both. The comparison tends to be at the expense of the later sculpture because the changing ideal that it reflects is less elevated than the one that produced the Parthenon.

The changing ideal, even more marked in the female figures (*Figures 6-8*), is most obvious in the progressive revelation of the body. Male nudity was acceptable to the Greeks from the first, but the strictures upon women in the

Figure 12

13

earlier civilizations demanded that their representations be draped. The bodies of *The Three Fates* (*Figure 14*) are described by clinging folds of drapery, which also serve to unite the figures in an unbroken, mounting rhythm, but they are neither revealed nor suggested as objects of allure or desire. When Praxiteles revealed the body of the goddess of love and beauty and exposed her as an opulently attractive woman in the *Aphrodite of Cnidus* (*Figure 8*), he ended a tradition. In the hundreds of variations on this statue (one of the fine examples is shown in Plate A2), the goddess is less and less a symbol, more and more a graceful, languorous, desirable woman. Here sculpture becomes more concerned with the superficial beauty that we can see than with the inner meanings revealed by physical beauty in the Golden Age.

There were, of course, reasons for this shift of values. For one thing, Athens had been badly shaken by military defeats. For another, her thinkers had examined the basis of a philosophy founded on acceptance of divine order and had rejected it for materialistic approaches. As a result, the serenity and inward unity of the Golden Age gave way to doubt and compromise, to what we call "looking at things realistically." The ideals of the Golden Age were tenable only in a limited and orderly civilization. Now the world invaded Athens;

the gods seemed less powerful, almost as if they had failed in their part of the alliance with man. Lofty concepts were affected by more mundane ones; inevitably Hermes and Aphrodite became more human than divine.

The Ideal Revived

With this background we may pause long enough to look at an example of the revival of the Greek ideal, as it was imagined to have been, by early nineteenth-century painters absorbed in re-creating the classical style. The late tradition of physical loveliness and attractive grace, derived from Praxiteles, was the basis of their neoclassical formula. There were two good reasons for this. First, the Praxitelean ideal is easy to understand, whereas that of the Golden Age is difficult for anyone without the time or training to enter the age vicariously through long and thoughtful study. Second, it was difficult to get at ancient Greece and its art. The first antiquarians came to know Greece once removed through Rome, where the ideals of early Greece were unknown or misunderstood; consequently neoclassical artists ignored or, rather, failed to understand the vigor of Greek art and its philosophical basis of joy in the world.

But if the Greek ideal was usually diluted and misunderstood, its most important aspect did remain clear to thoughtful artists—the concept of perfect order, complete in itself. This ideal is reflected in *The Funeral of Phocion* (Portfolio 7, Plate 76), an exquisite adjustment of a large number of individual forms in such harmonious order that the borders of the picture become the confines of a self-contained world. The artist, it may be recalled, was Poussin, a seventeenth-century French master who worked in Rome.

Rome was the haven and paradise of classically minded painters from Poussin to David. The city offered a double classical legacy: first, the monuments of ancient Rome itself, some of them derived from Greek proto-

types and all of them paying some kind of service to the Greek ideal of order, and second, the monuments of the Italian Renaissance, which had revived the classical ideal after Europe had passed through the experience of medieval Christianity.

Mars Disarmed by Venus and the Graces (Plate A3) is by Jacques Louis David (1748-1825), the leader of the neoclassical movement in the first years of the nineteenth century, when it was the international rage. After a series of "Roman" paintings in which he attempted to reproduce scenes true in detail and spirit to republican Rome, David decided that he wanted to be "more Greek." He relaxed the severity of his style, stripped his characters of their clothes, and generally abandoned the high moral tone of his early work for more superficial attractions. In *Mars Disarmed by Venus and the Graces* the god of war is nearly as graceful as a girl. He is a descendant of the *Hermes;* the slender proportions and small head follow generally the canon set down in the fourth century B.C. by the sculptor Lysippus, who discarded the one established by Polyclitus and formulated a new one in line with the taste for refinement. All the appurtenances in David's painting—the couch, the sandals, the shield and helmet, the pitcher and

cup held by one of the Graces—are as painstakingly accurate as David was able to make them by referring to his own sketches of classical fragments and by writing back to friends in Rome to ask for copies of this or that special bit of ornament. But if we compare his early paintings of Roman subjects with *Mars Disarmed by Venus and the Graces*, it becomes apparent that David held the mistaken notion that "Roman" meant strong and masculine and "Greek" meant graceful and feminine. He confused the purity of Greek art with affected refinement, its reserve with a sweet gentleness.

Washington Allston's *Italian Landscape* (Plate A4), an imaginary scene painted about 1805-08, shows us how the classical sobriety of the French masters was modified by the romantic attitude of an American. Allston, a young man of good family and education who made the grand tour to London, Paris, and Rome virtually required of every American intellectual in the nineteenth century, was determined to absorb neoclassical doctrines. *Italian Landscape* has obvious relationships to Poussin's work, but it is as romantic as it is classical, for Allston's dream of the ancient world was colored by the romance of being in a foreign land. He is as interested in the pic-

Figure 15

turesqueness of the Italian peasants he paints in the foreground (instead of the classically garbed figures to be found in a Poussin) as in the orderly architectural landscape behind them. He concocts his imaginary scene more from the point of view of a student thrilled by the adventure of travel than with the calm and analytical approach of a true classicist.

In Rome Allston saw the ancient world in ruins, even more so than we do. Many of the monuments were still half buried; vines climbed over them and shrubs grew in nooks and crannies of decaying stones. This romantic picturesqueness, entirely opposed to the classical ideal of order and completeness, influenced his concept of antiquity. The nostalgic vision of the ancient world overpowered the intellectual concept. The young American held Poussin and David as his ideals, but, unlike them, he was as much affected by the emotional character of romantic ruin as by the clarity and order of the classical ideal.

Not Gods But Men

In the final periods of Greek art, the balance continued to shift more and more in the human direction. Dramatic emotionalism necessarily replaced godlike reserve, for people had become more interested in sensations than in abstract ideas. The famous *Laocoön* (*Figure 16*), from about 50 B.C., shows how far the taste for melodrama was carried in sculpture. Every device of contortion and grimace is employed to elicit sensations of horror and anguish. The physical realism is untempered by idealism except in the most superficial echoes of earlier Greek forms. Most important of all, the *Laocoön* puts a premium on technical display. It is a fabulous piece of carving; the sculptor uses every trick of the trade with breathtaking skill. We are amazed—but we are not moved. We respond to the sculptor rather than to the sculptured work. When we look at the Parthenon figures or at the *Hermes* or the *Aphrodite*, we are primarily aware of the

created work and only incidentally of the technique of creation. But in the *Laocoön* the sculptor proclaims his own merit before he proclaims the nature of his subject (as Praxiteles does) or the nature of his idea (as the Parthenon sculptor does). Here is the final reversal of the abstract Greek ideal. The *Laocoön* will always be a popular work and in its own way a wonderful one, but it will never tell anybody anything much about the human spirit, no matter how dramatically it shows us that being crushed in the coils of sea serpents is an agonizing physical experience.

In a later age artists will use subjects of equal violence, pain, and suffering to express the turbulence of their own times or their own spirit, but it is difficult to read any such interpretation into the *Laocoön*. The sculptor has the whole range of technical dexterity at his command, but little to say. He is dealing with a legendary subject at a time when the legends had become only tales, not transmutations of convictions. He can do little more than illustrate the story of the revenge the gods took on Laocoön (a priest of Apollo who warned the Trojans not to touch the wooden horse offered by the Greeks) with all the polish at his command—as has happened again and again at the tag ends of great periods, when artists repeat the forms of a style without reference to the meanings they once served.

Rome

The *Laocoön* was carved three hundred years after the *Hermes*, so we have made a very broad jump from the first steps in the descent of the gods to their final coming down to earth. During these centuries Rome had succeeded Athens as the center of the Western world. (The terms Graeco-Roman and Hellenistic are used to describe sculpture executed in the waning Greek tradition but showing the influence of Roman taste.) If we have had any trouble understanding the Greek spirit, we should have none in putting ourselves in the

17

Figure 16

place of the Romans, who were so much like us in their worldliness, their love of everything big and powerful, and their cultivation of luxury and easy living in the days of Imperial world power that followed the more severe early days of the Republic. The Romans solved the problems of living in ways we still use. The Colosseum (*Figure 17*) was such an expert solution to the problem of getting thousands of people in to a spectacle, seating them, and getting them out again that we have been unable to improve on it as a functional plan and still use it as the model for our stadiums. As an architectural conception it is the opposite of the Parthenon, which we called a gigantic piece of abstract sculpture with no practical use. The Parthenon is full of extraordinary subtleties having nothing to do with utility. The steps, for instance, arch slightly upward in the middle, an all-but-invisible refinement that gives an impression of greater supporting strength and avoids the optical illusion that the heavy columns rest on a sagging base. The

columns themselves taper upward in a curved line, giving them a buoyancy, a life, that keeps them from being just so many stolid shafts. Every part of the design shows similar adjustments, so that the Parthenon, even in ruins, has more life than many a recent bank or post office modeled after it but designed in a simple, exact fashion.

The Romans, in adopting the Greek temple scheme, were more interested in size and ornateness than in this subtle perfection. Rome's contribution was made in buildings like the Colosseum and others serving a practical civic purpose. The Romans, like ourselves, tended to think of culture as an enjoyable addition to life, something to serve as a diversion for those with the money and the time for impractical things. In Greece the arts had been indivisible from the substance of life itself, but in Rome they were somewhat divorced from it. For the Greeks, sculpture had almost always been votive in nature; the Romans had an insatiable appetite for sculpture as sculpture. There was storytelling sculpture, commemorative sculpture, and just plain ornamental sculpture. When such great quantities as were demanded by the Romans are involved, there is always a great deal of routine hackwork; we hear almost as much about Roman vulgarity as about Greek purity.

In one field, portraiture, the Romans developed Greek sculpture in their own way, in exactly the way that might be expected, with direct, unidealistic reference to the subject and a forthright, skillful reproduction of his features. The *Kouros*, while it is a monument to a specific Greek athlete, is not a portrait in the usual meaning of the word. An ideal, not an individual, is represented. One of the few early Greek portraits making specific reference to an individual is that of *Pericles* (*Figure 18*) by Cresilas, from the Golden Age. Pericles was a man of late middle age when the bust was executed, but his wrinkles and his probable irregularities of feature, all such surface incidentals, are ignored. Tactful flattery was not the reason

18

for these omissions and improvements; rather, the portrait was intended to reveal the greatness of the inner man instead of the accidentals of his appearance. In the fourth century B.C., when Alexander the Great sat for the sculptor Lysippus, and even later, when portraiture flourished in Hellenistic sculpture, coins, gems, and paintings, the tradition of idealized likenesses was modified but not abandoned. It remained for the Romans, preoccupied with the literal facts of the world, to show men, women, and children with complete realism, feature by feature, as in the portrait of an unknown Roman (*Figure 19*). The Romans were so faithful to factual incidentals that it is possible to date some pieces within a few years by such transient vanities as the style of a woman's hair-do.

Since our brief survey of several centuries of sculpture began with the statue of an athlete, it might appropriately end with one, giving us a measure of the distance we have covered and the transformation of ideals that has occurred. The *Kouros* was an athlete who was half god; the Graeco-Roman *Boxer* (*Figure 20*) is a muscleman who is half brute. His battered head turns as if he hears some sound nearby. The attitude is as transient as that of the *Kouros* is eternal, in keeping with the later sculptor's world, where daily human values replaced the conviction of man's oneness with the forces of his universe. The *Boxer* is not idealized, nor does it pretend to represent convictions no longer held. (Its date, by the way, is about the same as the *Laocoön's*.) The sculptor sees the poor brute for what he is. If this body symbolizes anything, it may be the defeat of the human spirit through the buffeting of forces beyond its comprehension.

Figure 17

19

Figure 18

But the *Boxer* is a masterpiece. If we must measure it against the sculpture of the great periods before it, we say only that it is a masterpiece produced in a world that no longer permitted the transcendent serenity of the Parthenon sculptures, that no longer felt the joyous confidence animating the *Kouros*.

Echoes of Classical Painting

We have been discussing sculpture alone, as if painting did not exist in ancient Greece. It did. We have documentary reference to the great painters of the time and admiring comments on their work. (We know that painters, including famous ones, applied color to sculpture.) But hardly a flake of one of their paintings remains. From Tiryns we have fragments of a wall painting executed earlier than 1400 B.C. They reveal, in subjects related to religious observances and games (*Figure 21*), a style of great dash and vivacity, giving us an idea of the nature of archaic Greek painting. Greek

vase painting is available from all periods. It was a specialized minor art necessarily subservient to the nature of the decorated object, but it may reflect lost wall and easel painting. We illustrate a vase from the late Archaic period showing the god Poseidon fishing (*Figure 22*). The Etruscans, a vigorous pre-Roman people whose archaic sculpture is similar to that of Greece, have also left us numerous well-preserved painted tombs of the fifth century B.C. that suggest the styles of Greek vase painting. (Vases, being small and portable, could easily have reached the Etruscans, to whom, of course, the great Greek wall paintings would have been unknown.)

We have one fairly direct echo of an important mural painting of about 310 B.C., *The Battle of Alexander and Darius at Issus*, in the form of a mosaic version executed about 100 B.C. (*Figure 23*). All we can tell from it, allowing for changes inevitable in translating it into mosaic and other changes at the hands of copyists, is that the original must have been a

Figure 19

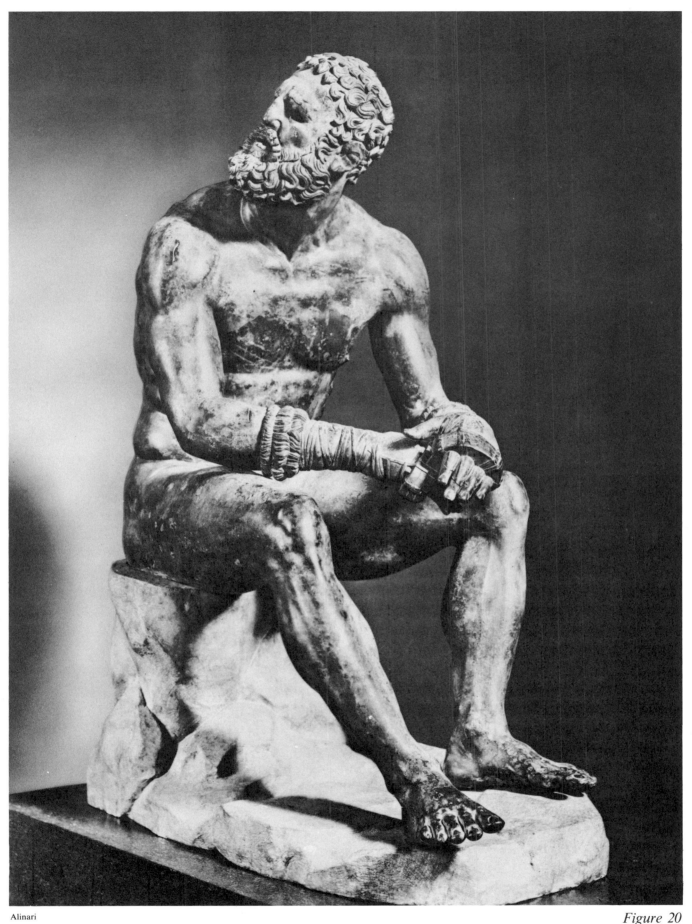

Figure 20

21

well-organized picture full of the emotionalized values found in the sculpture of the same period.

In short, we must guess at the nature of Greek painting. We know it had a realistic basis, as sculpture did, but stories of men trying to pass through painted curtains and of live birds pecking at painted fruit are dubious and tell us nothing about the way the great Greek painters, like the great sculptors, must have fused realistic form with expression of the Greek ideal.

What we do have is a quantity of Roman or Hellenistic painting preserved, paradoxically, by the eruption of Vesuvius that buried the cities of Herculaneum and Pompeii under vol-

canic ash in 79 A.D., and an occasional fragment here or there that has even more miraculously escaped destruction. *The Aldobrandini Wedding* (*Figure 24;* detail, Plate A5), which is named for the cardinal who acquired it after its discovery in 1605, was painted in the first century A.D. It is one of the most famous and influential paintings of antiquity because it was one of the first to come to light. It has been copied by Poussin and other painters.

The Aldobrandini Wedding probably came from a small room in a villa, where it was incorporated with decorative elements like festoons or garlands of leaves and flowers. The friezelike composition is organized into three sections representing different rooms in a

Figure 21

Figure 22

Figure 23

house, though these divisions are not allowed to break the continuity of the scheme. The painting combines rather literal, intimate, even informal realism with allegory and manages to unite human emotionalism with some of the abstract monumentality of the Greek tradition.

The central group shows the bride, a white-robed figure seated on the nuptial couch, with Venus, who places one arm reassuringly on her shoulders, at her side. It is apparent that the goddess of love is explaining things in a comforting and affectionate way to the uneasy young woman. The combination of very real human emotion with religious or allegorical reference is particularly successful here, where one might easily overpower the other or make it seem out of place and a little absurd.

The bronzed youth seated at the head of the couch is Hymen, the guardian deity of marriage. Alert to the progress of Venus' conference with the bride, he is ready to summon the bridegroom to the chamber when the goddess tells him it is time. On the left, completing the central group, is a young woman pouring scented oil. Her partial nudity indicates that she also is a goddess of some kind. The bride, as far as human companionship is concerned, is alone. We might believe that we

see her thus in the bridal chamber, after the completion of the marriage ceremony, during a moment of meditation or dedication at this dividing hour in her life.

In the alcove at far left a woman tests the temperature of a basin of water with a gesture so natural that it evokes the action as we have seen it hundreds of times. This intimate and housewifely function is probably being performed by the mother of the bride, in a space representing a small dressing room or retiring room off the nuptial chamber. At the right side of the picture the chamber gives onto an open vestibule occupied by three women. One of them pours incense. Another, with a lyre, sings the epithalamium, or marriage song. The third wears a crown; she may be some kind of ceremonial supervisor.

The symbolical narrative of the frieze is clarified and, above all, dignified by the nicely calculated relationship of the figures. The variety of pose and spacing characterizes them as individuals and avoids the monotony that is always a danger in a long, friezelike composition. The succession of verticals, the verticals of the figures echoed by those of the spare architectural background, suggests the dignified movement of a solemn procession. The painter, as he carries us slowly across the

Figure 24

space, rejects any temptation to introduce unnecessary incidental items that would have increased the superficial interest of the picture at the expense of its expressive dignity.

Cycle Paintings

The most spectacular Greek paintings were the *megalographiae*, which covered entire walls, frequently of great size. Ordinarily they depicted historical or legendary events that had a grandeur of theme appropriate to the dimensions. They must have been the pictorial parallels of the sculptural compositions on temple pediments. Their Roman descendants are found in rooms with a continuous frieze painted from floor to ceiling around all four sides. We have already seen a segment of one of these Roman cycles from a villa in Boscoreale (Portfolio 8, Plate 92). But one of the finest cycles, the frieze of the *Dionysiac Mysteries* (detail, Plate A6), in what was once a private Pompeiian villa, is still relatively intact. Bright even today, the walls must have been stunning, all but overpowering, in their original condition.

We are not certain whether the room they decorate was a living room or one reserved for the performance of the ceremonies pictured on its walls. Against a flat red background, nearly life-size figures enact the progressive stages of the initiation rites of a cult dedicated to Dionysus, god of wine and of the general fertility of nature. (In *Figure 5* we saw Dionysus as an infant, in the company of Hermes, who originally held a bunch of grapes for which the little god of wine was reaching.) The rites are shocking by our standards, involving flagellation of the neophyte as a prelude to an orgiastic initiation. But we must remember that what would be a debauch by one standard was part of the worship of fertility by another, one in which human procreation was included as part of the veneration of nature.

From the general view of the room given here (*Figure 25*), one may gain some impression of the compositional mastery of the unknown painter, although the full effect can be experienced only by standing in the room surrounded by the powerfully integrated frieze. What we have suggested about the processional quality of *The Aldobrandini Wedding* is true here too, but the composition is more complicated, involving as it does not only more figures but also incidents of greater variety that must somehow be brought into unified harmony.

With so large a scale and so tempestuous a subject, the mural would have been disastrously violent, bringing the walls crashing in on us, if the painter had not exercised the greatest discipline in the design and organization of his forms. The curve of a scarf or the swelling of a robe is reduced to a firm geometrical arc (Plate A6). Each figure is severely delineated and modeled with the solidity of an

24

architectural element. The background is divided into rigid rectangular areas that not only set off the curves and diagonals played against them but define the episodes of the narrative. Perhaps exceptionally strong colors were adopted in order to intensify the design, which might otherwise seem too quiet for its subject when disciplined by such architectural strictures. Altogether, the frieze of the *Dionysiac Mysteries* is masterfully conceived and executed.

Poetic Painting and Still Life

Roman painting had a wide range, from intimacy to monumentality. Some styles were characterized by meticulous rendering of detail, with almost the quality of miniature painting; others were sufficiently loose and free in execution to be described as impressionistic, with details eliminated in favor of rapid suggestion of the object as it existed in light and air (*Figure 26*). Fantasy was popular, and interest in pastoral nature, celebrated in lyric poetry, inspired poetically imaginative landscapes (*Figure* 27).

The delicacy of small decorative panels like one from the first century of our era, *Young Woman Picking Flowers* (Plate A7), sometimes

called *Primavera*, contrasts with the monumental decision and the geometrical severities of the frieze of the *Dionysiac Mysteries*. The softly fluttering draperies, so different from the firmly patterned ones of the Dionysiac figures, are enough in themselves to indicate a difference in spirit. And the touch of the painter is light, fresh. He is not a skilled draughtsman: the outstretched arm of the goddess (if she is a goddess) is awkward, and certainly the hand plucking the flower is no masterpiece of drawing. But these shortcomings are counteracted by the genuine charm and grace of the figure, stepping so vivaciously against the flat green ground. She is a worthy predecessor of the *Primavera* (Portfolio 5, Plate 58) of Botticelli, a renaissance artist who, incidentally, was so interested in the classical world that he tried to re-create from historical descriptions one of the most famous Greek paintings, Apelles' *Calumny* (Portfolio 11, Plate 122).

Some of the most charming bits of Roman art are found in details or individual panels showing still life, always a favorite exercise with painters. Still-life panels of food, plants, dishes, and birds ornamented dining rooms or loggias off gardens. Food shops and butcher shops had still-life paintings that shared the

Alinari

Figure 25

25

Figure 26

functions of signboard and wall decoration.

In connection with *Apples, Pears, and White Mug* (Portfolio 2, Plate 20) we noted that the eighteenth-century French artist Chardin, through his fascination with the textures of objects and his feeling for their inherent quality, lifted still life out of the realm of pure exercise and related it to philosophical experience. It would be an exaggeration to say that *Still Life with Eggs and Game* (Plate A8), a fetching Pompeiian still life from the Villa of Julia Felix, has the same revelation of the dignity inherent in simple things, but the artist does take the greatest pleasure in contrasting the burnished metal of the jug (to the right in our detail) with the texture of the eggs and in contrasting both these textures with the soft feathers of the birds. He cleverly fills the large perspective oval of the bowl with an echoing cluster of ten small ovals, the eggs; he enjoys the opposition of the outward swell of the body of the pitcher with the inward curve of the vessel on the left. He accents this vessel with a ladle balanced on its rim. The ladle's bowl repeats the oval of the eggs, whereas its thin straight handle relieves the full-rounded shapes of the other objects. The strict angularities of the stand on which they rest and the broken silhouette of the birds provide a contrast without which the other shapes might appear a bit monotonous. All these elements are represented in a limited palette of warm tans and cool grays, with bits of modified white, so that a group of commonplace things becomes a painting of much distinction.

Mosaic

If the Romans had an insatiable appetite for sculpture, they had a comparable one for pictorial images. To judge from the ruins of Pompeii, pictures were included on every bit of wall space an owner could afford to decorate. In addition, floors were covered with pictures and patterns in mosaic. A mosaic may be made of bits of colored stone or glass or other materials, such as shell, pressed into some kind of cement to bind them together. The durable surface was a practical necessity for floors, where painted designs and pictures would wear and wash away, but mosaic was enjoyed for its own sake and was used to cover walls and ceilings as well. We have already mentioned one example, *The Battle of Alexander and Darius at Issus* (*Figure 23*), translated into mosaic from a Greek painting.

Now, obviously, a painting translated into mosaic loses the subtleties of tone a painter achieves by blending one color into another or by modeling with very small strokes. On the other hand, mosaic has attractions of its own, the texture, the special colors afforded by marble and glass, their sparkle or polish. We can imagine how *Still Life with Eggs and Game* might appear in mosaic translation: the curves of the vessels would be less subtle, since the edges of mosaic pieces are sharply defined; softly blended passages like the feathers of the birds would become liney; light and shadow on rounded surfaces would be represented in bands of graduated shades. The over-all tendency would be to flatten, tighten, and simplify all shapes. An extreme example is the Pompeiian mosaic of a dog (*Figure 28*) where these problems are solved in the most direct way—by ignoring them and reducing the

Alinari

Figure 27

image to a silhouette. But what might have been nothing more than a crude indication of an animal has been made into an attractive pattern and an expressive image by the designer's eye for ornamental shape and his deft talent for capturing the essence of a subject with minimum descriptive detail.

At the other end of the scale from the direct, vigorous simplicity of the dog we have small mosaic panels like *Doves* (Plate A9), a translation into mosaic of painted forms similar to those in *Still Life with Eggs and Game*. In this case the tesserae (as the individual pieces of mosaic are called) are extremely small, since the aim is to approximate the naturalistic effects of painting, and the smaller the pieces, the closer this approximation can be.

Doves is a particularly fine example of what are called *emblemata*, miniature mosaic copies of popular paintings, usually surrounded by mosaic borders of geometrical or floral patterns. It comes as close to painting as mosaic can, and as a tour de force of this type it is a fascinating and beautiful novelty. But in the end, its virtues and its appeal come from the fact that it *is* a mosaic, a work of art with its own quality as an independent technique, as should be apparent if *Doves* is put side by side with *Still Life with Eggs and Game*.

Doves comes from the villa of Emperor Hadrian, located not far from Rome, which must have been the most elaborate and gracious habitation ever constructed by an individual for the cultivation of the good things of life. The little panel was designed to be seen at close range, treasured for its exquisite fineness of execution. But when mosaic covers an entire wall instead of several square feet, the task of applying millions of tiny bits of stone and glass becomes monumental. It has been done; in Saint Peter's, in Rome, there are tremendous pictures from the seventeenth century executed in mosaic. The tens of thousands of people who see them every year usually mistake them for paintings, especially since they are so high on the wall that the eye cannot perceive the individual tesserae. But

Alinari

Figure 28

27

Figure 29

except in these late and essentially freakish examples, the mosaicist with large spaces to cover worked with larger tesserae, with consequently greater differences between the style of painting and the style of mosaic.

Christian Mosaics

The art of mosaic reached its richest development in the first centuries of the Christian period. Technically, the Christian mosaics were descendants of the Roman ones, but a great change had taken place. The essence of the change is that mosaic no longer sought to imitate painting; its esthetic character was determined altogether and frankly by the inherent characteristics of the material and technique. The artist recognized that he was working in cubes of colored material with their own beauty, their own adaptabilities, and their own limitations. Many effects of painting had to be sacrificed, but each sacrifice carried a corresponding gain, especially in combination with the flat, simple forms of early Christian architecture. Mosaics are the glory of these buildings; the slight irregularities of surface catch and reflect light at different angles, giving the wall a wonderful richness, a glow and shimmer that painting cannot approximate.

The unrealistic style imposed by mosaic technique has a further importance in Christian art. As the world of pagan antiquity faded into the Christian era, men's attention shifted from the effort to achieve perfection in this world to the hope of eternal bliss in the next one. Christian thought was based on the idea of mystical revelation; the things of this world constituted obstacles in the way of a spiritual goal. Realistic art was inappropriate to this concept. There was also uneasiness concerning the second commandment, which forbade the making of graven images. The use of an image unrealistic enough to become more a symbol than a reproduction of an earthly being seemed permissible. So, instead of the full-rounded volumes of *The Aldobrandini Wedding*, we have

flat, linear effigies like *Saint Agnes* (Plate A10). A detail (*Figure 29*) shows the exact size of the tesserae making up the pattern of the figure, one in a procession of female saints carrying crowns, from a sixth-century frieze in the church of San Apollinare Nuovo in Ravenna (*Figure 30*). Instead of the illusion of space we have gold backgrounds, which, if they suggest space in any way, suggest the golden otherworldly space of heaven.

If we were attempting to present a detailed history of art, we would have to go into all the complications of the various mosaic styles, including some that continued to follow classical style more closely than the ones we have just seen. We would follow, thereafter, the subterranean course of art during the Dark Ages, when men all but lost the fruits of Greece and Rome. But since we are concerned only with mainstreams, it will be sufficient to say here that during this darkness there was a brief ray of light in the ninth century under Emperor Charlemagne, one of the most remarkable characters in history. Under Charlemagne, learning and the arts came very nearly into flower once more. A single example of manuscript painting from the period, *Saint Matthew* (Plate A11) from the Rheims Gospel, will serve to remind us that while the world seemed to have reverted to semibarbarism, the traditions of art and learning were still being kept alive, especially in monasteries, like small coals from which the flame would one day be rekindled. The next portfolio will summarize the art of mystery and faith of the Middle Ages, from the year 1000, when Northern Europe developed the second dominating element in our thought, to the edge of the Renaissance, with its revival of the ideals of antiquity.

The Persistence of Antiquity

We are so surrounded by imitations, derivations, and legitimate descendants of the ancient world that within a few feet of most people who read these words there will be a

Figure 30

molding on a cornice or a piece of furniture that would not exist if the Greeks had not invented its ancient ancestor. The coins in your pocket are derived from Greek and Roman models; the laws regulating your life come in part from Roman ones; the political philosophy guiding your life had its germ in Greek thought. And the majority of the forms of painting and sculpture as we know them, and the ideas expressed by them, can rarely be altogether dissociated from ancient ones. We will see this again and again as this second series of Seminars continues. As a conclusion to this one, it is appropriate to see one form this influence has taken in our century, with Giorgio de Chirico's *The Poet and His Muse* (Plate A12) as the example.

Chirico was an Italian whose boyhood was spent in Greece, where his father was an engineer, and whose first important painting was done in Paris. Classical influences were, therefore, pervasive in his development: he was affected by those of Italy, both of ancient Rome

and the Renaissance, of Greece itself, and of Paris, where he was surrounded by the monuments of the classical revival. *The Poet and His Muse* is an odd mixture showing classically garbed figures in an ordinary modern room; the poet sits in a shabby and certainly not very classical armchair in an attitude of contemplation while his muse bends toward him. The torso of the muse is composed of a mass of engineering and mechanical symbols, some modern, some as old as Euclid. The heads, abstract volumes inscribed with diagrammatic lines, are a reference, intentional or not, to the geometrical elements in classical art and learning. The picture may seem grotesque as a classical subject, and it certainly has its elements of affectation, but much of classical monumentality is still present. It is, at heart, a kind of personal charade in which a modern master of fantasy pays his particular kind of homage to the dream of the ancient world and recognizes its continuity in a century that seems to have departed so far from its ideals.

30

Color Plates

Figures in the Text

APHRODITE *Greek*   The Metropolitan Museum of Art

PLATE A3   MARS DISARMED BY VENUS AND THE GRACES *Jacques Louis David*   The Royal Museum of Fine Arts, Brussels

ITALIAN LANDSCAPE   *Washington Allston*   The Addison Gallery of American Art, Phillips Academy, Andover

Detail from THE ALDOBRANDINI WEDDING *Roman* Vatican Library Rome

Detail from THE DIONYSIAC MYSTERIES *Roman* Villa of the Mysteries, Pompeii

YOUNG WOMAN PICKING FLOWERS *Roman* National Museum, Naples

STILL LIFE WITH EGGS AND GAME *Roman* National Museum, Naples

PLATE A10   SAINT AGNES (copy)   *Italo-Byzantine*   The Metropolitan Museum of Art

SAINT MATTHEW *Carolingian* Pierpont Morgan Library, New York

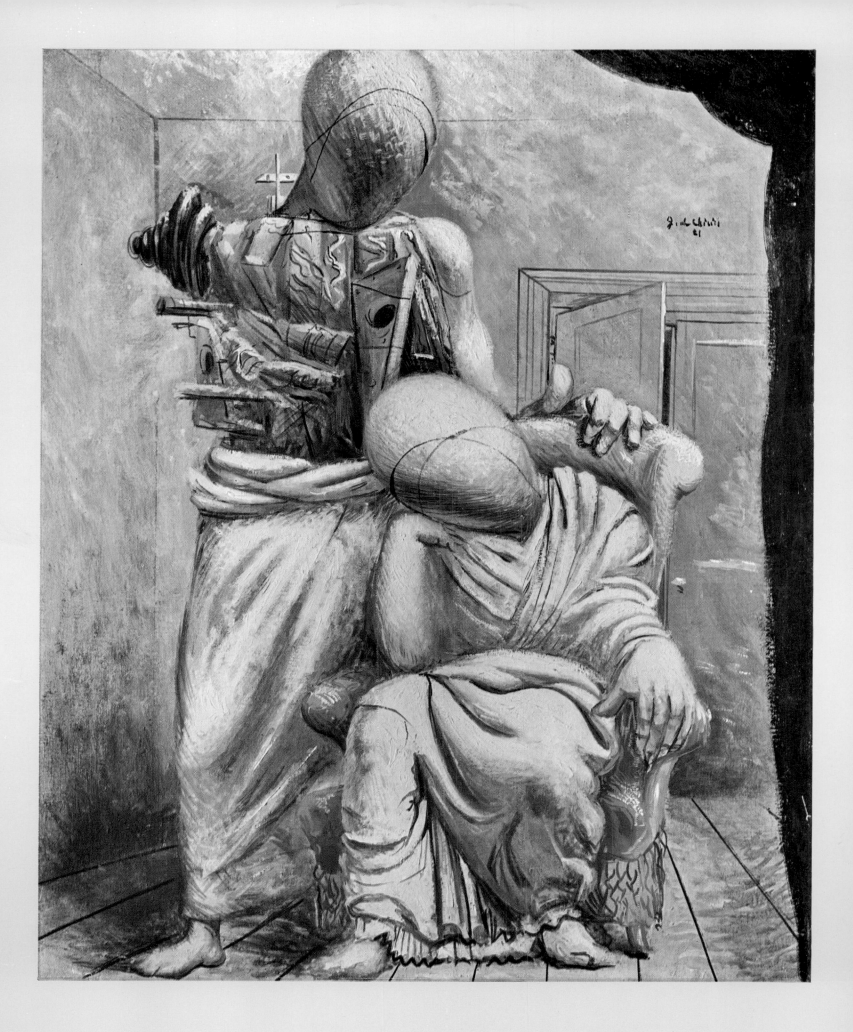

PLATE A12   THE POET AND HIS MUSE   *Chirico*   The Philadelphia Museum of Art